Digital Research Phrase Book

By:
Susan Louise Peterson

Digital Research Phrase Book

Susan Louise Peterson

CONTENTS

Preface...vii

Prologue ix

Acknowledgements...xi

Introduction..1

Chapter 1: Internet Research Phrases 3

Chapter 2 : Technology Research Phrases 13

Chapter 3 : Web Research Phrases..23

Chapter 4: Data Research Phrases 33

Chapter 5 : Cyber Research Phrases 43

Chapter 6 : Online Research Phrases....................................53

Chapter 7 : Virtual Research Phrases....................................63

Chapter 8: Network Research Phrases...................................73

Chapter 9: Email Research Phrases 83

Chapter 10 : Computer Research Phrases.............................93

Chapter 11 : Digital Research Phrases................................103

Chapter 12: Electronic Research Phrases 113

Recommended Reading 123

Index 125

Afterword..133

PREFACE

Years ago I started writing phrase books to help researchers and educators put their writing thoughts into some type of logical flow as they drafted their writing and research projects. However, over the last 20 years a new element of technology and the digital world has started to impact research writing. The **Digital Research Phrase Book** was born to help add technological types of phrases in the research and testing process. Writers from various academic fields can incorporate these phrases into their writing and research projects to gain a more virtual and technology based writing approach.

PROLOGUE

Some academic writers are really skilled in understanding the research guidelines for developing a proposal, however they may lack experience in technology and digital skills to stay updated in a more electronic given world. The **Digital Research Phrase Book** takes some of these research principles and combines them with online and cyber ideas to form digital research phrases. Undergraduate and graduate students, as well as professors, academic professionals and university staff can use these digital phrases in forming research proposals, grants, articles and theses submitted for academic publications and university review committees.

ACKNOWLEDGEMENTS

I want to thank my past education and multidisciplinary professors for making me aware of how important it is to watch how I phrase things in reports and academic papers. Their 'watchful eyes and expert editing' skills gave me new things to look at as I wrote papers in the university setting.

I want to thank my husband for his technology insight as he uses cyber technology on a daily basis in the schools. He has provided me with an array of web and online resources to help me build my digital knowledge and incorporate it into my research and writing. My daughters are also a 'thankful' part of my life as they show mom how easy it is to navigate the computer and internet as if it was just a click of a button. I wish them the best in their journey into college and the adult world.

INTRODUCTION

Academic writers sometimes delve into understanding the research process for a particular topic or idea they want to pursue. However, when the topic needs to be more technology in its focus these same writers cringe as they lack digital skills to explain research in more computer or web based terms. In the **Digital Research Phrase Book** many of these academic testing and research phrases are rewritten with a more virtual, computer and internet quality. The aim of the **Digital Research Phrase Book** is to provide phrases with more virtual, web based ideas that can be incorporated into academic writing on a variety of topics.

CHAPTER 1

INTERNET RESEARCH PHRASES

the research results were tracked on the internet

a research timeline was developed on the internet

global internet challenges were addressed in the research

internet research tools were used to

the challenge of internet research is

the internet was utilized for the literature review

internet research themes were noted in the report

a research guide was presented on the internet

the desktop was used to customize the internet research results

a series of research topics were searched on the internet

internet access was approved to collect the research

research subjects had internet access of

internet searches were utilized to research the

internet access was provided to research subjects

an internet survey complimented the research

the internet was used to design an online research conference

research images were added from the internet

internet investigations expanded the initial research

a research manager collected ideas on the internet

the purpose of the research was described on the internet

research groups were formed from the internet

research information was included in the internet presentation

internet problems were noted in the research

internet resources were provided as part of the research

research participants navigated the internet

the internet was used to find research maps

internet research tools were displayed

research directions were posted on the internet

a comprehensive research design was shown on the internet

the internet was used to locate research articles on the

research subjects kept a journal on the internet

the internet allowed more research collaboration

the historical research project was documented on the internet research periodicals were categorized on the internet

research patterns were shown on the internet

research rubrics were developed on the internet

research productivity was documented on the internet

internet resources enhanced the research problem solving

ethical research issues were noted from the internet experience

an internet model facilitated the research

research forms were distributed on the internet

a scientific research project was conducted on the internet

the research responses were monitored through the internet

the research investigation was designed on the internet

the internet recorded each research response

internet research questions were formulated

the internet was used to gather information

research data was analyzed on the internet

each research explanation was analyzed on the internet

the research model was designed on the internet

the internet was part of the research tools

research predictors were noted on the internet

internet descriptions were emphasized in the research

research explanations were highlighted on the internet

an internet explanation was coupled with the research

a research inquiry was made through the internet

each research explanation was included on the internet

research results were tallied on the internet

research accuracy was verified on the internet

the internet provided a technological research design

research theories were posted on the internet

each internet research weakness was mentioned

internet advances helped speed up the research

a new internet research project was developed to

internet research ideas were implemented by

differences in the internet research project included

a new research phenomenon was indicated on the

internet research questions were presented on the internet

the benefits of internet research include

each research design has an internet focus

research questions were revised on the internet

the proposed research design was put on the internet

an internet solution helped to implement the research

a consequence of the internet research design was

the research model was revised on the internet

an internet designed solution was proposed for the research

similarities were noted in the internet research project

a historical research perspective was presented on the internet

internet innovations were included in the research

the internet search was broad

each internet survey contained five questions

internet research gained in popularity

the internet was used to narrow the research topics

internet computer topics were research

internet themes were used to focus the research on

internet results were analyzed in the research

internet research was challenging in that

research noted internet problems by

the important internet issue of

the research results were tabulated on the internet

an open internet approach helped encourage research responses

research weaknesses were noted on the internet

a historical internet approach was presented in the research

each internet topic presented new research questions

internet research areas were limited to

the research hypothesis was internet related

the purpose of the internet research was to

each internet question opened new research possibilities

internet research will continue to be a focus of study

research modifications were proposed on the internet

proposed internet designs were implemented in the research

research criteria was confirmed on the internet

each internet research objective has a different purpose

internet examples were proposed for the research

the internet provided various views of the research

the research design was supported by the internet

internet evidence was noted in the research

internet modifications helped built the research

internet advances helped contribute to the research study

the internet provided alternative research solutions

research contributors were identified on the internet

traditional research approaches were analyzed on the internet

research explanations were modified on the internet

research predictions were built into the internet

an internet evaluation accompanied the research

the internet research was compared and contrasted to

research theories were examined on the internet

a research assumption was developed on the internet

specific internet problems were noted in the research

internet resources were noted in the research

each internet research approach had

internet issues were discussed in the research

research concerns noted the internet problems

subjects had limited internet research access

research themes were internet related

internet research aids were utilized to

internet research articles were formatted with

research results were calculated on the internet

the main internet research focus was

internet research searches reviewed numerous studies on

internet instructions were given prior to research collections

the internet was used to enhance research information

each internet research question was developed from

the research publication was available on the internet

a question and answer format was part of the internet research

the research gained popularity from the internet

each internet hypothesis was addressed in the research

the aim of the internet research was to

internet research included many facets such as

internet access hampered the research

the internet hurt the confidentiality of the research study

internet research needed university approval

a committee approved the internet research approach

research was focused on internet topics

internet has changed the research focus

research was formed from internet issues

internet problems interfered with the research

internet issues clouded the research

research participants signed on to the internet

an internet research phase was developed

each internet approach was researched

an internet research focused study was needed to

each research topic was internet focused

internet concerns were used to form research questions

research problems focused around internet use

some internet research was disregarded

internet responses varied in the research

each internet response was coded in the research

internet research issues raised future questions

CHAPTER 2

TECHNOLOGY RESEARCH PHRASES

technology was used to conduct research observations

each research plan explored a technology issue

research prompts had a technology element

technology inservice training was included in the research

research results were shared with technology

research gaps were noted in relation to technology use

technology was implemented through the research

the technology helped promote research on

research feedback was collected through technology programs

technology helped complete the research as a faster pace

technology was an important part of the research

research effectiveness was noted by technology

a research portal was designed with the technology

the research vision changed when technology was introduced

technology competence skewed the research

technology was the tool for one research goal

each research concept was planned with technology

the research was more purposeful with technology use

online technology helped speed up the research

technology was a welcome addition to the research

the panel conducted technology research visits

the technology research program was voted the

technology research terms were presented

each technology visit had a research purpose

the research approach involved a specific technology

researchers were vocal about the technology

technology was paramount to the research

volunteers were incorporated in the technology research project

the research incorporated the latest technology

technology teams monitored the research

staff with technology research skills were trained to

specific technology approaches were related to research

technology problems impacted the research outcomes

a corporate grant funded the technology research project

some technology glitches slowed the research

the research required specialized technology

research projects introduced technology to young adults

each student had a technology research topic

technology research topics were judged on

the research process involved technology

research materials included a technology component

a technology tool utilized in the research was

technology was utilized in the research model

a technology model was used in the research

the research explanation was constructed with technology

the research design was developed with technology

technology was used to brainstorm research ideas

a technological research model was used to

research questions were formed with technology

research responses were organized with technology

technology resources facilitated the research

the research investigation was technology based

technology was used for the research peer evaluation

research solutions were formed with the help of technology

each research decision used a form of technology

each research response was coded with technology

technology was used to collect the research data

technology was used to explain the research model

the research experiment incorporated technology to

technology was used to document research responses

technology tools were assessed in the research

research information was presented with technology

relevant technology research topics were identified

each research technique included technology to

technology resources were included in the research

technology terms were explained to the research participants

a technology explanation was used to describe the research components

technology principles became part of the research

research issues were identified with technology

research tools included the technology use of

each research investigation had a technology focus

participants needed technology training to complete the research

varied technology approaches addressed research issues

research design options were created with technology

the research itinerary was developed with technology

research inservice training helped explain the technology

technology professional development was part of the research

research observations were recorded with the technology

technology was combined with the research components

adopted technology standards were used to research

the paper focused on ethical technology issues

technology applications were explored in the research

technology information was directed to societal issues

technology resources were applied in the research setting

results were analyzed with a technology method

research topics were generated from technology issues

the technology researched looked at attitudes of

the research technology was compatible with

a number of technology resources were identified

a community technology center was used to

technology based tools were part of the research project

technology was used to facilitate data collection

instructional technology practices were combined to research the

responsible use in technology research was emphasized to

technology was used to retrieve research data

a technology model was developed to

technology was utilized to locate subjects for the study

the technology research was applied to

the research and instruction was technology based

research technology terms were defined as

technology was used to modify the research design

a technology survey in the research explored attitudes of

each student researched and created a unique technology approach

the effectiveness of technology use was researched to

there was a lack of technology utilized in the study

technology research audits were conducted to

the research project was organized from technology categories

the technology was meaningful to help explain the research to

the research used a technology skill checklist to

technology integration was observed in the research

school technology plans were researched to establish

the technology used for the research assessment included

a research graph was developed with technology to

the value of this technology research project came from

research participants rated their own technology skills to

the research technology project concluded

a technological summary of research problems were identified to

technology connections were identified in the research

technology differences were noted in the research

the research benefit of using technology was noted

each technology issue was addressed in the research

a review of technology plans was part of the issue

technology features were the center of the research

technology concerns were overshadowed by the research

technology staff supported the research project

additional technology staff were needed for the research

technology maintenance became a research issue

a technology grant was needed to finish the research

technology results were impacted by the research flaws

technology issues were raised frequently during the research collection

research concerns had a technology focus

limited technology skills slowed down the research results

the research directors had technology certifications

the technology results were supported by the need for further research

each research subject was pre-screened for technology skills

technology research resources were limited to

the technology research project was noted for

the primary technology sources for the research was

each research paper had a technology theme

the technology research was expanded to include

technology results were used to focus the research study on

the research hypotheses focused on technology

technology was the focus of the research study

the research mission had a technology theme

each technological research study had

a technology goal was presented for each research objective

technology setbacks slowed the research

technology teams covered different research aspects

the technological research project was awarded to

there were financial limitations for the technology research study

the research conclusion is discussed in relation to technology

the technology summary was research focused

research limitations were directly related to technology

in summary, the technology research project lacked

each research phase had a technology element

the research plan included technology features

the research thesis contained a technology component

technology must be added to the research procedures

technology terms were defined in the research

technology limitations were discussed in the research

CHAPTER 3

WEB RESEARCH PHRASES

equipment was restored to the web research lab

web research questions were answered in a timely manner

the web research program was restructured

the web research conference had many speakers

a good source for web research was

the web education forum was opened to the public

it was a difficult web research matter

web research collection resumed on

recent web research decisions impacted the

adjustments in the web research project were reviewed for

the results of the web research survey found

web research concerns were listed in the report

the web research schedule was revised

web researchers were resourceful to find the

the board was responsive to the web research needs

a response was made to the web research request

the web research problem resurfaced

the web research case was settled

a full web research agenda was developed

the specific details of the web research project included

web competence was noted in the study

a web-based research design was used

the website had a research evaluation component

a research interpretation was presented on the website

the research is on going on the website

research scores were linked into the website

computers were aligned with websites

a web based approach was used to research

the internet increased the website research exposure

research concerns were posted on the web

research staff members were encouraged to use the website

web based practices were researched to

a research portal was available on the website

the website listed the research procedures

each research assistant had a website

the website engaged participants in the research

a centralized website was used to collect research data

multiple research methods were shown on the website

each research model was web based

websites were assessed for research compatibility

a customized website was used for the research

the research justification was described on the website

the researcher designed the website to

the purpose of the research was described on the website

a website was used to evaluate the research

alternative websites focused the research on

the website provided five research strategies to

the website prioritized

the research decision was evaluated by web results

a weakness of the research was noted on the website

the website was developed to store the research information

web problem solving was utilized in the research

the research results were evaluated on the website

research conclusions were provided on the website

research priorities were listed on the website

the website noted research clarifications

the analyzed data was included on the website

research findings were summarized on the website

research strengths were identified on the web

a website was developed to explain the research

the website was monitored throughout the research study

research participation was calculated from website use

each website stressed a different aspect of research

research strategies were used to compare the websites

research progress was explained on the website

website content helped formulate the research goals to

research perspectives were explored on the website

the website provided a research scoring procedure

the research focus was announced on the website

each website research question was answered

the research rationale was explained on the website

research activities focused around the website

relevant research issues were listed on the website

each web survey was scored for the research study

the research experiment had a website focus

a national research project was designed on the web

the current status of the research was reported on the website

the website listed meaningful research to

the research feedback was explained on the website

the research was re-evaluated on the web

research subjects had access to the website for

the research website was use to analyze computer literacy on

research conclusions were posted on the website

the research design was implemented on a website

a research strategy was proposed on the website

each webpage focused on a different research question

a web application was formatted for the research study

the website enabled the research subjects to

research graphs were available on the website

the website provided a research training model to

the research focus of the website is to

the website listed the research testing procedures for

past and current research was linked to the website for

the research website reinforced the

a comprehensive website facilitated the research by

the webpage stressed the importance of the research

a website was used to tabulate the research results

each website was used to collect research

research results were displayed on a website graph

each research survey was completed on the website

research questions were posted on the website

the website listed the research procedures for

use of existing websites was

graduate students collaborated on the website

the data was processed on the website

a series of web projects was used to research the

creating a research website was important for

the research website introduced the

research connections were linked to the website

a research webpage was put on the website

a website approach was used to screen the subjects

there was a website attack on the research network

the website provided research enrichment activities

a website was created to collect research

the website contained research tools for

a research website project was developed to

each web project had a unique research focus

research informational queries were developed from a website

website problem solving activities were researched

a research questionnaire was placed on the website to

the web design was displayed

each research web component was addressed

web research was expanded in several areas

web pages focused on various research issues

web challenges were common in the research project

website research issues were prevalent

web research questions were rewritten for

research methods were web based

a full research website was developed

website scoring procedures were simplified

web posts brought up new research issues

web approaches varied to collect research

the website had research safety features

a security feature was added to the research website

web surveys contained additional research information on

websites needed revamping for

a new website designed enhanced research collection

the websites were not compatible with data collection sites

each website was reviewed monthly

a common website research issue was

specialized training was provided for web researchers

the web research incident was described in detail

speculations were made about web research

web research involved a series of steps

the strength of web research was

the department struggled with web research

web research efforts were challenged by

the web research issues were studied carefully

a web research study was conducted on

there was a full examination of the web research complaint

substantial changes were made in the research web design

a solid web research program was developed

subjects made suggestions for improving the web research

helpful hints came from the web research project

new web research ideas were considered by

the main points of the web research were

details noted on the web research were distributed to

supplemental web research materials were developed

a written description of the web research incident came from

a web research syllabus was designed for

CHAPTER 4

DATA RESEARCH PHRASES

participants were emailed data research information

data research transitioned to

the new requirements for data research included

research consultants were contracted to help with data collection

support for the data was provided in the research

data was reorganized for the research studies

an article addressed important data research issues

compromises were made to complete the data research project

researchers directly supervised data collection

a steering committee oversaw data collection for the research

data research policies were revised

multiple research departments contributed data

the data was used in a pilot research study

there were conflicts with the research and data

each data collection project had a research manual

funds were earmarked for data research

interest was generated on the topic of data research

mistakes were pointed out in the data research

educational materials were developed with data research

the researcher was an expert in data collection

a trial data collection was used to train the

collaborations on the data supported the

a data review was concluded

benchmarks were established from the data

each research group reviewed the data

many assumptions were made from the data

a consultant helped explain the research data

research data was designated into categories

a critical part of the data was

observations were made about the data collection

a credible company was used for data collection

the data evoked researchers to

students had different ideas about the data

the data reinforced the idea of

students were preoccupied with one aspect of the data

data reinforced the research idea of

the data provided borderline results

the research data bridged a gap between the

in a nutshell the data consisted of

a remarkable aspect about the data was

a consequence of the data collection was

the data collection procedures were outlined

the data was checked for accuracy

a summary of the data provided research information

researchers made statements about the data

mistakes were identified in the data

a corrected copy of the data results was distributed

the data was put in a new research format

the data provided a detailed description of

the data was modified to research the

each research department collected different data

data was revised to address different research issues

the research data supplemented the

the university supported the data collection

the data collection was arranged to

students were not accustomed to this type of data collection

administers supervised the data collection

the bureau had concerns about the data

data collection was stressful

data collection was slow

an established data base was utilized

the test format varied as data was collected

a brief part of the test shared data results

the data was used in the test results

a research database was selected to

computerized research data was collected

the data was collected in a controlled setting

three data research projects were analyzed

data collection was achieved with special test arrangements

research data was developed in digital format

the testing standard for data collection was

digital directions were developed for the data collection

the data corresponded with

data was collected electronically

the data and testing scores were reviewed

viable electronic research data was used to

a benefit of data review was

data driven assessments were used to research

the highlight of the data collection was

a student led research group collected data

the purpose of the data was to

release of the data and results continued to be slow

the data prompted researchers to look at

the data was confusing for

the data aided the researchers to examine

the data was ambiguous

advice was given to research assistants on data collection

data was disseminated to

counselors helped with the research data

a testing advocate spoke about the data

claims were made about data collection

graduate assistants were unprepared to use the data

the media criticized the data and testing procedures

the data was disputed

a decision was made to use the data for

associations wanted access to the data results

the test analysis found the data could be

an alternate form of the test was used for data collection

researchers chose to omit the data

the data was examined and the results were released to

investigators determined the data was

data confused the research participants

permission was obtained prior to data collection

clues helped in the data collection

data was monitored and checked for

data is reviewed annually

time was allotted for data collection

a petition was made to address data concerns

the data collection took several weeks

funds were appropriated for data collection

teachers supported the data being used for

the research data was adjusted to

each year data is collected to adjust the

the data collection was approved by the board

there was some apprehension about the data

the data provided unique information

a feature of the data collection was

researchers were urged to question the data

data was randomly collected

data was categorized by grade levels

data research was used to start a new approach

research was highlighted in the data collection

data from the research spotlighted on

data research was used in the field investigation

research participants looked for the data

data collection reviews were held daily

a weekly data collection was analyzed

the data research pool was divided into

research data was examined for changes

data was an important component of the research

one problem highlighted in the data collection was

the biggest problem area for data collection was

data varied from different geographic areas

demographic data was analyzed in the research

data was collected monthly

the data results were stronger during the

the concert interfered with data collection

adjusted data was sent to the director

a review of the data collection procedures was completed

data was used to understand the underlying reason for

a combination of data collection techniques were used to

there was an urgency to collect the research data

the number of data research participants increased

a straightforward data collection approach was used in the research

researchers explored the possibilities of data expansion

a significant factor in the data research was

the research project brought a national focus to the data

a fundamental part of the research data was

the data was joined to another research project

researchers were obligated to share the data

an online notebook stored the research data

detailed notes were keep on research and data facts

the data collection policy was objectionable

data research highlights were not accurately described

the data provided candid information on research topics

the previous research data was altered

a mistake was overlooked in the research data

the data resulted in research curriculum changes

each data research project was unique in

the researchers grappled with the data

CHAPTER 5

CYBER RESEARCH PHRASES

students expressed concerns about the cyber research project

a review team observed the cyber research

the researcher planned to address cyber issues

the aim of the cyber research was to

current trends in cyber research include

there were many aspects of cyber research

inservice training was provided on cyber research

cyber research projects were developed to

a review of the cyber research noted

there were many challenges with cyber research

improvements were made in the cyber research project

a cyber report was presented on the research

a unique aspect of cyber research is

a literature review was completed on the cyber research

cyber research results suggested

the cyber research was evaluated for

the cyber research was recognized for

cyber research had an impact on

cyber research was debated

cyber research classes focused on

a cyber research study emphasized that

the cyber research program was monitored for

cyber research curriculum consists of

the cyber research survey found

cyber research programs are diverse

a limitation of cyber research was

a cyber research checklist was helpful to

there were many opinions about cyber research

cyber researchers were advised to

the intention of cyber research is

a cyber research workshop enhanced the

the cyber research schedule included

the objectives of the cyber research program were

cyber research responded poorly to

a legal aspect of cyber research was

the cyber research study concluded

the purpose of the cyber research is to

cyber research support was limited

the regulations for cyber research call for

a historical fact of cyber research is

research cyber links were disorganized

one essential part of the cyber research was

the cyber link emphasized important aspects of the research

a cyber research referral was made to

a committee was formed for research links

cyber links helped the research participants by

a professor chaired the cyber research committee

cyber research procedures were updated

the committee determined the cyber research guidelines for

the focus of the cyber research class was to

the cyber research rights were explained

revisions were made for the cyber research project

each subject was given a cyber research packet

the cyber research packet contained parent information

consent was obtained for the cyber research

some subjects refused to participate in the cyber research

one task of the cyber research committee was

the cyber research department was contacted by

cyber field trips were part of the research

an annual review of cyber research found

cyber computer links were established with the research

the cyber research was linked to

legal issues were linked to cyber research topics

a report linked the cyber research components to

special education agencies were cyber linked to the research

the research consisted of cyber links to

different research was cyber linked to new topics

a commission cyber linked the research to

the research screening was cyber linked to

there was a reaction to the cyber research links

the cyber research ruling was linked to

an adaptable cyber link was developed in the research

the cyber linked research was a lengthy process

there were cyber research classes linked to areas of study for

the cyber research links were evaluated for

a cyber linked extension was formed for the research

the cyber linked research was classified under

some cyber research issues were linked together

the cyber research links were expanded to include

the cyber researcher concluded the links were good for

college students benefited from the cyber research by

cyber research has its origin in

subjects needed help in cyber research procedures

assistance was provided for the cyber research project

an appropriate cyber research program suggestion was

cyber research subjects were usually

a cyber research specialized program was developed to

each cyber research participant signed the petition

the objective of the cyber research was

the cyber research in schools shows that

an important aspect of cyber research was

a decision was made to halt the cyber research

cyber research specialists were hired by the district

the cyber research participants requested

cyber instruction is provided for

some advantages of cyber research include

cyber research was conducted in the home environment

instructors were sought for the cyber research project

cyber research strategies were developed to

it was essential for the cyber research project to include

cyber research was safeguarded from

a new edition of the cyber research test was

cyber research concerns were ranked by

cyber research results were checked thoroughly by

educators criticized cyber research

research staff reviewed the cyber instrument

financial support was provided for cyber research

the subject suspected a problem with the cyber research

changes were made in the cyber research project

researchers reflected on the use of cyber techniques

the cyber research program operated under

an abstract of the cyber research was presented

cyber research was supported by the university

there was a wealth of cyber research on the topic of

the biggest challenge of cyber research is

cyber research administrators were sought to

the primary cyber research concerns were

the role of the cyber researcher was to

a cyber research presentation was made to

a rough draft of the cyber research found

cyber research benefitted the university

cyber research had an international focus

the cyber research had stumbling blocks

cyber researchers focused on the

the credibility of cyber research was questioned

cyber research was used for part of the study

each research participant had a cyber experience

cyber researchers were pulled in several directions

cyber research interest grew

cyber research was considered a new field

the cyber research project had a two-fold purpose

the three major components of cyber research were

cyber research was considered a new approach

the university objected to the cyber research proposal

new cyber research issues were suggested by

cyber research had new considerations for

cyber research changes were common throughout the project

a common cyber issue was

cyber research was allowed for the grant

each project had a cyber research focus

the cyber research field was changing

a controversial cyber research topic was

there were different ability levels in the cyber research course

an effective cyber research method was

the cyber researchers were skillful at

cyber research was structured to

the cyber research assessment found that

the qualifications for the cyber research position were

a new cyber research technique suggested that

there was a mismanagement of cyber research funds

the funding for cyber research was cut

cyber research students gave an account for

the area of cyber research study includes

cyber research accommodates the

the cyber research faculty collaborated with

the equipment was adapted for cyber research

cyber research was lacking in some departments

according to the cyber research guidelines

the cyber research project faced unique circumstances

action was taken by the cyber research department

CHAPTER 6

ONLINE RESEARCH
PHRASES

the research team agreed on the online questions

an online assessment meeting was scheduled to

a disadvantage of the online assessment was

a debate resulted from the online testing

the online test version was discontinued

the credibility of the online test was questioned

online test items were grouped by

online test data was discussed

a series of online tests was used to

a critical point of the online test was

the online test emphasized the area of

a frequent online problem was

selected professors reviewed the online test for

online test results were unclear

the online testing report indicated

online testing documents were saved to

the difference between the online tests was

research assistants guided the subjects through the online tests

plans were made to postpone the online test

some staff opposed the online testing

a reserved online test was posted on

the design of the online test featured

the online test was extended to include

subjects had a good outlook about the online test

online test failure was a concern

researchers had a choice of online tests

the online test session was accelerated for

online tests were ranked for

a fallacy of the online test was

clarification was needed for the online items

a favorable aspect of the online testing session was

misunderstandings of the online testing were addressed to

several articles were rewritten on the online testing

each school collected the online tests

a combination of online tests was used to evaluate

a panel designed the new online test

teachers were appointed to the online testing board

the administration encouraged online testing

online test performance was reviewed by

some students were excused from the online testing

an online research conference was planned for

it was evident from the online test

only a few online test problems were identified

online test results were calculated by

a subject was exempted from the online testing

online test results were disputed by

online test emphasis was put on

one online test score was disqualified

the online approach was initiated by

a drawback of the online testing was

researchers eagerly awaited online test results

an online testing symposium was presented by

early online test results were discouraging

outdated information was eliminated from the online text

the outcomes of online testing were discussed to

the conditions for the online testing were

the online test situation was hindered by

the online test contained illustrations of

the online test commentary helped to persuade

the reasoning behind the online question was

the online test was constructed to examine

the online assessment discouraged subjects

the online instrument called attention to

online testing problems were discovered

the online test included a direction booklet

dialogues were exchanged about the online research

each online quiz included an answer key

it was difficult to concentrate on the online test

online test outcomes were compared to

the online quiz was rewritten

a prospectus for the online test was mailed to

the online testing idea originated from

online testing was required to

subjects were uncomfortable with the online approach

an online test was used for the competition

subjects had the opportunity to take the online test

online test questions were refined

online testing results fluctuated

corrections were made for the online version

the district made important online research decisions

online research funding was an issue for

a director was hired to coordinate online research

the online research department was relocated to

the rally supported online research

the online research folder was misplaced

extra supervision was needed for online research

the online research files were reviewed quarterly

a routine was developed for the online research

weekly adjustments were made in the online research

the main issue for online research was

online research students were introduced to

the chairperson was influential in developing online research

two online research classes merged

the staff assistant helped maintain the online research program

mistakes were made in administering the online research

online research proceeded to

corrections were made on the online report

online research was designated

the conduct of the online researcher was appropriate

each online test evaluated a different academic area

the online test was well received

an online test hearing was scheduled to

a team of researchers supervised the online process

it was determined that the online test was

online assessments were directed by

the online test procedures were repeated

the online test was given intermittently

a number of online tests were incomplete

each college conducted their own online testing

a notice of the upcoming online test was distributed

the online test was given sequentially

online test results were anticipated

the online regulatory board had concerns about the

the online test examined social skills

a visual online test was used to assist

the administration provided online test supervision

there was some online test bias

there were some online test obstacles

opinions varied on the online testing procedure

the online test was pretested

online results were analyzed for

an online sample was studied for

each online instrument was scored for

the online research was summarized in

a literature review was completed online

online participants contributed to the research

online research was fast and effective

an array of mistakes were made in collecting the online research

online research grew in the department

an online post test was given to

an important aspect of the online research was

the main challenge of online research was

some online research questions were deleted

a research committee approved the online research

students were introduced to the online research project

a practice online test helped research participants gain confidence

a support group answered the online research questions

online research scores were categorized by

each online research participant was interviewed for

the most prevalent factor in the online research was

the online research was misinterpreted

participants were notified of online research changes

there were misconceptions about online research

the focus of the online research shifted

details were omitted from the online research

the online research complaint was withdrawn

participants were mislead by the online research

the online researcher was faulted for

wrongdoing was found in the online research project

the equipment was adjusted for the online research project

it was a model online research facility

reforms were made in the online research project

classes duplicated the online research model

the more complicated online issues were addressed first

a processing issue was addressed for the online research

the online research was paramount to

the aim of the online research shifted

the online research director was reassigned

a multitude of online research problems were noted

CHAPTER 7

VIRTUAL RESEARCH PHRASES

virtual research information was important to the study

a virtual research survey initiated a need to

there were virtual resources needed to research

there were group discussions on virtual research

virtual research problems needed special attention to

virtual research classes were determined by

computer problems impacted the virtual research results

students wanted information on the virtual research project

a virtual research seminar helped prepare

a special virtual research program was designed to

virtual research personnel were identified

some research participants were given assistance in virtual techniques

the speaker presented on the topic of virtual research

certain skill training emphasized virtual research

problems were corrected on the virtual research project

researchers cooperated with subjects in the virtual research study

a current list of virtual researchers was developed to

the subject had trouble concentrating on the virtual research screen

virtual research projects were combined to

the experts in virtual research were knowledgeable of

new virtual research training classes were developed

subjects needed help to master virtual research techniques

subjects had many obstacles with virtual research

technical experiences were provided with the virtual research

a virtual research seminar was held at

subjects needed assistance on some virtual research procedures

a critical evaluation was completed on the virtual research project

additional virtual illustrations were provided for the research

staff needed additional training on virtual research techniques

virtual skills emphasized research approaches

virtual research classes resumed

there was tension in some virtual research groups

virtual research problems were noted

virtual areas of interest were studied in the research

questions were formulated on virtual research issues

virtual research was displayed by

there was some flexibility in the virtual research pages

the staff brought attention to virtual research

it was considered a model virtual research program

a major part of the virtual research program was

the definition of virtual research includes

virtual resources were placed in a folder

virtual techniques were used to research the specialized area of

virtual research procedures were explained to

virtual research topics were debated

one technique hampered the virtual research

the consequence of virtual research was

researchers were accountable for mistakes in the virtual project

problems with virtual research could have been presented to

the university was responsive to the idea of virtual research

a repercussion of virtual research was

the virtual research compelled others to

some evidence promotes the use of virtual research

the department had a history of conducting virtual research

virtual research files were re-examined

the subjects had problems with virtual research

a virtual research problem was overlooked

there were restrictions on using the virtual research

the results of the virtual research revealed

the focus of virtual research emphasizes

characteristics of virtual research include

the virtual research process consisted of

the virtual research project was rescheduled

virtual research activities helped students relieve stress

there was an analysis of the virtual research

students are in need of a virtual research project

this area of virtual research is controversial

a virtual remedial framework was researched

virtual research participants were identified by

recommendations were made for improving virtual activities

the origin of virtual research includes

specific virtual research goals were established

graduate students planned a specific virtual research program

administrators examined the virtual research chart

virtual activities were planned to

a review of virtual research found that

virtual classes were added to the research schedule

a weakness of the virtual research project was

the criterion for virtual research consisted of

a determination was made about the virtual research

virtual research was coupled with

a virtual research time table was used to show

the criteria for virtual research included

a virtual sample was drawn for the research project

the subjects received virtual research support

virtual research workshops were held to

the scope of virtual research was

virtual research examples were developed to

details of the virtual research plan were shown to

there was no doubt about one virtual technique

a detailed virtual research plan contained

the scope of the virtual research project was

a combination of virtual research approaches were used to

attitudes toward virtual research have changed

virtual research classes supported the research project

the extent of the virtual research project was

there was a search to recruit virtual research participants

the virtual research class centered on

it appeared to impact the virtual research

today's view of virtual research is

virtual research had a flexible component

the researcher became an advocate for virtual research

the virtual research department was deemed inadequate

an annual review was conducted on virtual research

an agreeable decision was made about the virtual research

recognition was given to the virtual research program

the conclusion on virtual research was

a limitation of the virtual research was

a plausible solution for the virtual research was

the university board had some reservations about virtual research

there was a modification on virtual research

the virtual research goals were attainable

the deadline for the virtual research project include

the virtual researcher's action was questionable

the decision of the virtual research committee was acceptable

a shortcoming of the virtual research project was

a virtual research group participated in a joint project with

there was a workable solution to the virtual research problem

the rationale behind the virtual research was

virtual researchers responded with

virtual research was complicated for some research subjects

each virtual research section had

parts of the virtual research emphasized

virtual research was reviewed for issues related to

the virtual research components were presented to

the board approved the virtual research project

virtual issues were addressed in the research

virtual problem areas took time to correct

correction for virtual research mistakes was slow

virtual research problems were common in the project

a support class helped answer virtual research questions

virtual research confidence was low

research subjects lacked virtual experience

virtual research interest started to increase

a project addressing virtual research issues was developed to

the virtual researchers struggles with the answers

the biggest problem for virtual research was

undergraduate students had a positive virtual research experience

graduate students were involved in the virtual research project

there were space limitations for the virtual research equipment

the virtual research project was terminated

the researcher had limited virtual research experience

each virtual research project had different objectives

the department chair had reservations about virtual research

there were barriers in the virtual research

there was a review of the virtual research paper

a letter supporting virtual research was written by the chair

there was a virtual research task force

the virtual research was blocked by

there was insufficient information on the virtual research

an auditor reviewed the virtual research concerns

it was apparent more assistance was needed on the virtual research project

the virtual researchers goals were attainable

several students witnessed the virtual research incident

staff received literature on virtual research

assistants recorded virtual research observations

journals in the area of virtual research were provided to

a virtual research graduate student developed a project to

a virtual research grant provided funds to

CHAPTER 8

NETWORK RESEARCH PHRASES

a mandated part of the network research was

a necessary part of the network research is

network research was utilized for

additional network support was provided for the research

network restrictions were imposed on the research

after a careful network review, research changes were made

network research was aligned with

a transfer of network research results was complete

network space was utilized for the research

network guidelines were reviewed with research concerns

network research information was reported to

the state had network research guidebooks

it was inevitable the network research project had problems

the network consultant was authorized to stop the research

a layout of the network research provided

under the research conditions, the researcher was asked to

the network approach was inventive for the research

the original network research concept was developed by

researchers were organizing the network to

a network narrative explained the research

the first research objective will be to network with

the network helped present the research practices

three research techniques were utilized on the network

an alternative network was used for the research

research choices were provided on the network

researchers needed more skills to use the network

the research process was included on the network

the researchers acknowledged problems with the network

identified networks were used to collect research

no specific research method was used on the network

the network was used to discuss research needs

the research influenced participants to look at the network

research was embedded into the network

measurable research changes were viewed on the network

the relationship between the network and the research was

the technology of the network was complicated for the research

the network was effective for collecting research data

research experience hindered the use of the network

the network helped with building the research design

the network met the state's research standards

the evidence-based research was put on the network

the benefits of network research are

the reward of the network research project was

the research was implemented in the network setting

the network minimized the research collection time

subjects were responsive to the research network approach

a weakness of the research was the network process

the research network was used across settings

the research indicators were presented on the network

the network provided for research skill practice

the research was reinforced by the network

the network was the basis for research choices

the research was combined with network areas

clear research expectations were explored on the network

the network model helped to draw attention to the research

each network was managed by a research administrator

the network maintenance tasks enhanced the research

a natural consequence of the research network was

a deficit of the network research project was

research subjects were coached on how to use the network

the rationale behind the network research project was

research probes were exhibited on the network

research cues were provided on the network

a research hierarchy was formed on the network

the network research results were generalized to

the network set up target responses from the research

research steps were listed on the network

the research was replicated on the network

the network provided ways to make research decisions

the research conditions were set up on the network

research prompts were used on the network

the major point of the network research project was

researchers based decisions on the network use

the research network was not beneficial for

each network provided a unique research setting

the network was used to provide research implementation

the effects of the network research were

the problem with using research networks is

research participants did not understand the network

some participants responded better to the network research project

the network research process involved

the research team recommended a network approach

the network system of research focused on

a research characteristic of the network was

the principles of network research include

the network approach provided evidence based research

research network strategies were developed to

the network research process was compared to

network research was implemented by

the intensive network research consisted of

the network research attempted to

there was a compromise on the research network

a graphic displayed the network research

a consequence of the network research was

frequent research opportunities were available on the network

a more effective network approach to the research would be

the network tools were utilized for the research

security procedures were reviewed for the network research

the most frequently visited network research programs were

the network application was installed to research

research choices were allowed on the network

research assistance was provided on the network

frequent research opportunities were available on the network

an effective network complimented the research

research input was available on the network

the research focus was allowed on the network

each network was designed to research the

an effective network enhanced the research

the research context was presented on the network

research descriptions were clear on the network

the network was used to collect research on

the network provided a way to score the research

a specific research technique was part of the network

the network was accountable to calculate research results

relevant research procedures were outlined in the network

research variables were identified on the network

complex research questions were put on the network

each network provided research directions

the network allowed for research consistency

the network presented the research expectations

networks provided a challenge in conducting the research

each university had a unique network for research

networks varied in research efficiency

research data collection was hampered by the networks

some networks had problem areas in completing the research

some research networks had limited maintenance

one network did not allow the research program

an overview of the network was conducted prior to the research

research networks were developed to pinpoint the

research goals were not reached in some networks

networks not functioning correctly were omitted from the research

network problems plagued the research

the network was corrected to collect the research

each network had different research challenges

the network joined computers were used to collect research

a joint network was designed for the research

the network was developed for a specific research purpose

each network was set up for research participation

one research network excelled in collecting subject responses

the network was not directly used in the research study

the community showed support for network research

there were many viewpoints about network research

positive comments were made about the network research

parents were angered by changes in the research network

the overall image of network research was

the network format was altered in the research

network regulations were simplified in the research

the pace of network research moved quickly

progress was made in changing network research guidelines

network research must adhere to

a small percent of parents agreed with the network research results

the public's perception of network research was

insightful remarks were made about network research

a weekly network research newsletter was created

the network research publication focused on

researchers had different network perspectives

a network research petition was designed to

the basic philosophy of network research was designed to

one area of network research was formatted to

the network research was part of a pilot program

CHAPTER 9

EMAIL RESEARCH PHRASES

email objectives were modified to

the email was implemented by

a deliberate attempt was made to email all participants

the email research notification was flawed

the email outcomes indicated

email responses were reinforced with

some students mastered email participation

the email verified the

the email routine was practiced with the subjects

subjects cooperated with the email schedule

the email routine was practiced for several days

the email served to enhance

the researcher demonstrated the email to

the email was primarily used for

the email addresses different learning styles

specific email skills were tested

the graduate students were trained in email strategies

email results were listed in the

inservice training helped explain the emails

there were different objectives for each email

the email was given on an ongoing basis

email compliance was monitored

email results were explained in the grant proposal

email school wide testing indicated

the staff had more dialogue about the email

broad email participation was encouraged

email performance was evaluated by

an email handbook was developed to

email scoring was delegated to

the email policies included

email comments were supervised by

a staff development specialist explained the email

staff were recruited to help in the email process

a panel addressed the email issues

a psychologist administered the email for

subjects with special needs were emailed the

curriculum activities were emailed

the email format varied at each university

the emails were aligned with testing

the district supported the email

students were encouraged by the email

a portion of the email was omitted

the email agenda was reviewed with

the email was reviewed in a journal

email scores were recorded by

teachers pointed out the email lacked

the email content was reviewed

the email was praised by research subjects

the email was aligned with the curriculum

the email publication was examined

an essential part of the email was

the email was sent at various intervals

students had different email experiences

similar emails were compared

a like form of the email was used

email testing periods lasted about three minutes

the email tally was completed

an email glossary was provided

assistants tabulated the test results of the email research

email participation improved by using

each email was connected to the subject area

a researcher commented on the email approach

the goal of the email format was to

there was evidence the email was ineffective

the email agitated some research subjects

email had a big influence on

some subjects rushed to open the email

the email was inapplicable

email was delayed to some research subjects

a tutor helped type the emails

the intent of the email was to

a substitute email was used to

email connections improved the research by

classes helped prepare subjects to answer emails

the proposed email was reviewed by

the email was integrated with

credit was given for answering emails

students were interviewed about the email

a preliminary email was sent to

an email itinerary was passed out

subjects were given time to answer emails

the email interaction was positive

email documentation was used to form a

email surveys were used to collect research for

emails helped in getting research results

each email had a research focus

research results were dependent on emails

an email reminder helped to collect more research

the email was addressed to research recipients

email confidentiality was a research issue

emails were confusing for research subjects

the email was misunderstood in the survey

research utilized emails for demographic information

email responses disrupted the research

there was a lack of email participation in the research

research was slowed by unanswered emails

incentives were given to complete the email research

emails gave ideas for further research

emails proved to be helpful in the research

the email was poorly written and confusing

email standards were established by

administers managed the emails

each unit had an email survey

the student received an email waiver

an exit survey was emailed to

the email demonstrated how

email committees were formed to

only research subjects had access to the email

the emails were related to various themes

emails were sent out at the end of each semester

the director enforced email safety procedures

the email responses were kept private

some research emails contained private information

the email was monitored for safety concerns

research emails were only disclosed to

only researchers were allowed to see the email results

research subjects could only access two emails

a technical monitoring system was used for the emails

privacy rights were explained regarding the emails

security procedures for the emails were reviewed

email support impacted the research

the research used different versions of the email

email was delayed in parts of the research

emails backlogged the research

an email was rewritten for the research

no emails were lost in the research

response rates were low in the email research project

incentives were provided to encourage email participation

emails contained easy to read research instructions

email research was reviewed for problem areas

the email research focused on two major aspects of

email results were analyzed for errors

research emails were approved by the university

the research committee objected to the emails

a new email was resubmitted to the university

each email had a different research focus

emails for the research were overlooked by the subjects

the email response rates were high in some areas

a lower email response rate was from older participants

the email research benefitted the university by

research emails were sent as follow ups to

a table illustrated email research responses

the bar graph featured email research results

the email research was an important contribution to the study

each email was coded for confidentiality

the email was used for data collection only

emails had a specific research purpose

email was used as a research gathering technique

multiple email approaches were used in the research

misplaced emails hampered the research study

emails both hindered and helped the research

an email research study was used to

research was email focused to specific

a group research email was used to

the email was unrelated to the research study

the subject of the email was to research the

the research summary explored different email topics

the email literature review included research on

email research supported the study by

email participation was needed for the research study

CHAPTER 10

COMPUTER RESEARCH PHRASES

the computer helped me to expedite research planning

a research backup plan was identified for computer failures

computers enable a broader research perspective

research information was placed on a computer backup disc

research content objectives were posted on the computer

the computer helped lay-out the research design

computers were used to implement the research

computer labs were used to collect research

computer integrated research was used to

each research participant was placed on a computer

computer equipment was purchased for the research

computer analysis was incorporated in the research

the computer provided flexibility in collecting research information

computer graphics displayed the research

the research goals were computer related

computer and internet policies were reviewed prior to the research

research questions were posted on computers

research participants were paired on computers

computer support was given to research participants

computer locations were identified for the research

the function of the computer research was

established practices were developed in computer research

a promising computer research technique was introduced

computer research training was given to teachers

graduate students received computer research training

the computer research programs varied

there are many different aspects of computer research

experts had varied opinions on computer research

in light of the computer research program

there were different views on computer research

computer research was judged on

the vision for computer research was

a vital part of computer research

computer research was impractical in that

a committee reviewed the computer research project

a panel investigated computer research problems

computer research is essential to

a violation of the computer research program was mentioned

a major criticism of computer research is

a disturbing fact of computer research

the computer was used to print the research inventory

research participants browsed the computer to

research scores were calculated with the computer

the research hypothesis was posed on the computer

research sites were bookmarked on the computer

each research component was investigated on the computer

research assistants searched for computer information

research subjects searched the computer for

research budgets were calculated on the computer

complex research questions were placed on the computer

research information was merged into the computer format

research conclusions were posted on the computer

participants scrolled the research on the computer

a research inventory was developed on the computer

research tables were designed on the computer

research subjects replied to computer messages

research participants had to double click on the computer

sound was added to the computer research project

each research subject browsed the computer

research patterns were displayed on computers

the collaborative research project utilized the computer to

a computer research approach was used

research observations were recorded on the computer

students emailed the research form from computers

the computer research helped predict the event

an informational search was developed on the computer

research was measured through computer programs

research participants were mentored on using the computer

each researcher posted preferences on the computer

computer searches facilitated the research

a research favorites option was posted on the computer

a research question and answer was generated on the computer

an electronic research list was computer generated

computer groups were formed to discuss the research

online research events were listed on the computer

the research project director was available for

research skill levels were assessed on the computer

research frequently asked questions were addressed to

the web browser helped to navigate the computer research

the research involved computer assisted instruction

each research computer was counted to determine

enable minor computer revisions for

the research was conducted on personal computers

the research subjects each logged on the computer

students responded to five computer generated questions

the computer research was integrated with

test responses were recorded on the computer

computer research definitions were noted

the computer scoring criteria was established

time was a factor in the computer research project

the computer test administration time is around 20 minutes

the computer items were updated

the research used a computer format

computers were used by research assistants for

computer research was used to calculate age

each subtest was computerized

each computer subtest was presented online

the computer research file was edited

the computer research program was halted

the research participants logged on the computer

research was retrieved on the computer

computer assisted research was explored to

a computer research slide show was developed to

computer education was part of the research

computer research was put into a column format

the computer was a research tool to

each research component had a computer graphic

computer prompts were given as part of the research

some research files were deleted from the computer to

the computer was used as one research method to

the research computer file was inserted in

a research file folder was placed on the computer

a computer search determined the research participants

a computer research template was provided

research percentages were documented on the computer

the computer was implemented to update research information

computer graphics facilitated the research

a duplicate research file was put on the computer

research information was arranged on the computer

major research points were summarized on the computer

computer lay-outs displayed the research

the computer research was questioned

permission slips were needed for the computer research

each computer was formatted with research questions

a computer link was developed for the research

research findings were posted on the computer

computer research began to spread to

a university computer lab was used to collect the research

results of the computer testing opened doors for more research

research was submitted on computer forms

research ideas were formed from computer results

computer problems interfered with the research schedule

one major computer issue setback the research project

computer support was variable in the research project

the goal of using computer research was to obtain

computer effectiveness was lacking at some research sites

computer programs lacked support in some research areas

the research was compromised by computer weaknesses

a special computer program enhanced the research

computer failure lost part of the research data

computer personnel lost interest in the research

the computer research team was formed to

computer researchers teamed up with

tam work was a big part of the computer research

the subjects developed their own computer research style

the computer research techniques were demonstrated by

computer research was transferred to

it was a big transition to go to computer research

the accuracy of computer research was questioned

a specific type of computer research was recommended

a comprehensive computer research program was designed to

computer researchers were upfront about

there was an upheaval in the computer research department

an up to date computer research report was developed

researchers were updated about computer changes

a plan was made to research and upgrade computers

subjects were upset by the difficulty on computer research

researchers were urged to gain advanced computer skills

the computer research materials were useful for

the computer research was revamped

more services were provided in computer research

CHAPTER 11

DIGITAL RESEARCH
PHRASES

digital screening tests were used to process

new word were introduced on the digital test

all facets of the digital test were discussed

the digital test was abbreviated

specific digital test sections were identified

students could use their notes on the digital tests

the digital research was facilitated by

a condensed version of the digital test was used

digital test worksheets were simplified

a visual digital instrument was suggested

step by step directions were prepared for the digital research

the digital testing and research was challenging

digital test interpretation was confusing

resource books were developed with digital testing

a digital research team addressed problem areas

a range of digital tests established the

a digital picture test was used to

short answer digital tests were used to

the digital test questions were arranged by topics

it was a realistic digital testing situation

the digital research was part of a pilot program

there were many opinions about digital research

digital research was devoted to

there was an ongoing review of digital research

the digital research was designed to accommodate

a platform of digital research included

a statement was made on the digital research policy

the digital research program was nominated for

the digital research program was controversial

staff was committed to the digital research program

the digital research program was noteworthy of

the digital research class was outdated

the digital researchers received a confidential warning

a detailed summary of the digital research included

a remarkable digital researcher developed

there was an important article on digital research

colleges promoted digital research

the goal of digital research was

digital research was demonstrated in a practical way

an established digital research method was used

the digital testing process included

the structure of the digital testing was to

a digital report described the testing results

a number of digital test suggestions were developed

the digital test focused on

digital research activities took place on

the digital researcher addressed the problem areas in

informal digital tests helped to prepare for

the digital research pinpointed certain problems

the digital testing workbook was useful for

a crucial aspect of the digital research was

digital test taking skills were reviewed

optional digital testing was provided to

digital tests were reproduced

a hands on digital testing approach was used

feedback was given on the digital research procedure

a significant part of the digital testing was

the digital research was practical for

a practical aspect of the digital test was

a teacher's assistant helped with the digital testing

an important feature of the digital research was

the digital test screening system indicated

digital test taking methods were debated

the digital research was used to verify

teachers selected one of two digital tests

the digital test was brief

the value of the digital research was questioned

some parts of the digital testing were optional

digital research was conducted at various levels

a series of digital tests helped to

digital tests were part of educational placements

some digital tests had similar features

the digital testing criteria included

the digital test was given in English and Spanish

a reliable digital instrument was used for testing

a digital testing session was held at

the digital testing process was summarized

the digital test packet contained score sheets

early digital test screening was used to

results of the digital test were kept confidential

a useful aspect of the digital research was

digital test illustrations were developed to

descriptive digital information indicated

the digital test was lengthy

software programs were utilized for digital research

a digital answer key was provided

the practical value of the digital research showed

the digital test version was difficult

the purpose of the digital research was

the scope of the digital testing included

digital research was reviewed

a sample of the digital testing results were studied

a single digital test was used

the digital test was translated

illustrations were in digital format

the digital test kits will be ordered

there were problems with the digital testing

the revised digital test concluded

the digital research environment was hampered by

the digital test results were misplaced

a digital test item analysis was conducted

a digital testing binder was put together

the digital test was understandable

the digital research procedure was simplified

the digital test reference gave additional information for

the digital issues of the testing were discussed

it was a nationally recognized digital test

a digital self test was given to the student

digital test scoring was complex

the objectives of the digital testing changed

the directory of the digital tests was provided to

digital test scoring patterns were reviewed

a digital testing profile was collected

digital testing printouts explained the results

the sample digital test was beneficial

the digital research experience was positive

teachers helped to determine the digital testing procedure

digital testing suggestions were offered to

the digital test was very detailed

the digital test completion time was

digital issues were common place in the research

each digital issue was addressed

a special feature of the digital research was

digital tests were adapted to

digital tests needed major revisions

digital profiles helped organize the research

the research analyzed digital results for

digital testing had some security issues

multiple versions of the digital tests were designed to

the digital test was designed to provide

digital tests were timed and scored

digital research emphasized the idea of

digital research explored the elements of

digital research steps were explained

digital research was being encouraged in graduate school

digital research goals were hindered by

a part of digital research involved

the digital research goals were unclear

the digital research explanation was bias

only some digital research issues were addressed

the digital research project was slightly altered

the details of the digital research project included

digital research made an appeal of

there was sufficient equipment for digital research

the politics of digital research included

a reference point of digital research was

digital research principles were applied to

a preview of the digital research was applied to

digital research discussion questions were collected

the future of digital research was uncertain

the digital research committee was productive

there were new digital testing requirements for the research

the procedure for assigning digital research subjects was

prompt action was taken on digital research complaints

it was a difficult digital research matter

recent digital research decisions were revealed

the digital research class was replaced

a reply accompanied the digital research questions

digital research concerns were listed on

the digital research provided a resource for

CHAPTER 12

ELECTRONIC RESEARCH PHRASES

electronic test scores were compared to

the electronic responses were computerized

the electronic test scores were plotted

the electronic test was a checklist to determine

concerns were expressed about the electronic testing

an electronic testing pattern was found

electronic research specialists reviewed the test for inconsistencies

an overall electronic test score was provided

electronic test information was provide for the research subjects

an electronic test identified problem areas

electronic testing booklets provided

electronic research directions were read by

the electronic test format included

electronic scoring was fast and easy

the electronic test examiners were trained

it was a supplemental electronic test

the electronic test results were in the research findings

electronic testing times were coordinated with schedules

electronic research guidelines were reviewed

the original electronic test was no longer used

electronic research notes were used to

research messages were sent in electronic formats

the research took an electronic focus

an electronic sample was obtained for the research

each research hypothesis was electronic focused

one major electronic research issue noted was

the research model was presented electronically

the research had an electronic scoring feature

different electronic features were used in the research

the electronic research version indicated

the research quoted electronic sources

electronic research was presented on a screen

an electronic screen presented the research data

each electronic research issue was addressed

the electronic research study concluded

each electronic issue was addressed by

electronic research results were confusing for

electronic research was fascinating for

each research participant had an electronic profile

the electronic research was overwhelming for some

electronic procedures were updated

the electronic test summarized the

the electronic test screened students for

individual electronic testing was administered

each electronic test item was timed

an alternative electronic research method was used

an initial electronic testing review was conducted

electronic testing results were computerized to

the electronic test manual helped to

researchers assisted in grading the electronic tests

each subject had an electronic test form

electronic testing arrangements were made for the

an electronic inventory of testing materials was developed

a variety of electronic test techniques were used

the electronic test was designed to screen for

the electronic test items were easy to score

one electronic test question was rewritten

the electronic test scores were totaled

the electronic test was administered to a group

an electronic pre-test was given early in the year

the researcher charted the electronic test results

the electronic test evaluated the

subjects participated in electronic post testing

the student was a candidate for electronic testing

the electronic testing components were listed

the findings of the electronic research concluded

the electronic tests had some weaknesses

the electronic test was timed

the strengths of the electronic test were noted

the research participant was referred for electronic testing

a portion of the electronic test was untimed

the electronic testing tool was given to

there were questions about the electronic testing

a battery of electronic tests were given to each subject

the electronic test objectives were shared

it was an easy to score electronic test

electronic test scores were interpreted by

the electronic instrument was field tested

electronic testing issued were discussed

electronic activities varied in the study

the subjects were given an electronic test to

an electronic setting was used for research testing

the electronic testing determined that

a special electronic feature of the test was used

subjects responded well to electronic testing

each electronic test was upgraded

electronic tests were administered in classrooms

a revised edition of the electronic test was used to

the electronic testing results were analyzed

different electronic levels of the test were administered

a comprehensive electronic testing program was recommended

electronic testing materials were ordered

the electronic test measured the areas of

a sample electronic test was reviewed with

an electronic testing form was developed to

a teacher administered the electronic testing

the electronic test version was utilized for

the electronic test contained comprehensive questions

electronic testing techniques were reviewed with

there was an electronic description of the test

the electronic testing scales revealed

electronic drawings were analyzed

the electronic research was scored

both an electronic and print version of the test was used

the electronic practice was developed to

items were selected through an electronic procedure

electronic research content was approved by the department

multiple subject electronic testing was conducted

electronic resources enable subjects to

different electronic learning activities were utilized in the research

research subjects were introduced to electronic resources

electronic technology was utilized to research the

an electronic research model was developed to

electronic messages were sent to research participants

research assistants had access to electronic information

an electronic innovation delivered the research to

electronic research result reports show

the electronic test scores were compared to

different electronic test versions were used to

alternate electronic tests were given

electronic research was enhanced with a special program to

one electronic research approach involved

electronic research is a changing field

a stumbling block in the electronic research project was

the electronic research approach that worked best was

each electronic research format was reviewed by

a sequential approach was used in the electronic research

the electronic research results were separated into groups for

the electronic feature of the research was found to be

the effectiveness of the electronic research was in the

electronic results were stored in research folders

each research study was electronically scored

one electronic approach centered around the research on

electronic steps were noted in the research

the lessons from electronic research came from

research steps were formed electronically

electronic research formats were used in conjunction with

each electronic feature was discussed in the research

the electronic research was overshadowed by

two electronic research approaches were contrasted

electronic research phrases indicated a need for

the electronic research focus centered on

research was based on electronic information

electronic scoring sped up the research

an electronic focus was needed in the research

electronic approaches to research were discussed

an electronic testing folder was distributed to

electronic research results were presented to

a computation error was noted in the electronic research

electronic research is needed to expand

an expansion of electronic research supported

research ideas were developed with electronic approaches

electronic research responses were confusing

electronic tools answered research related questions

each electronic research approach contained

a feature of the electronic research study was

each research project had unique electronic features

an electronic flaw was noted in the research

the electronic test form was revised

each electronic research study had limitations

RECOMMENDED READING

Peterson, S. (March 22, 2013-Kindle Version). *The Research Writer's Phrase Book: A guide to proposal writing and research phraseology.* Lanham, MD: International Scholars Publications.

*The Research Writer's Phrase Book (*available in both Kindle and print versions) helps guide research writers in the writing process as they start to develop research proposals and written research projects. The book contains research phrases on topics such as the purpose, objectives, need for the study, review of literature, methodology, conclusions, recommendations and implications for the study.

Peterson, S, (1998). The Educators' Phrase Book: A complete reference guide. Bethesda, MD: International Scholars Publications.

The Educators' Phrase Book: A complete reference guide is a book that contains phrases to help educators in their writing efforts. Some of the phrases cover topics related to curriculum, behavior, instructional and learning phrases, school planning and assessment, as well as teacher, principal and student phrases.

INDEX

A

Access, 3,7

Adjustments, 17

Advantages, 37

Analyzed, 18

Applications, 13

Approach, 30, 120

Assumption (s), 9

B

Barriers, 56

Bookmarks, 26

Benefit, 14

Borderline, 26

C

Centralized, 17

Challenges, 23

Checklist, 15

Clarification, 19

College, 46

Computer (s), 17, 93-101

Committee, 8

Compatability, 17

Competence, 9
Conclusion, 21
Content, 20
Corrections, 70
Criteria, 9

D
Data, 33-43
Data Collection, 33, 34, 36, 38
Decision, 17
Demographic, 30
Design, 6, 11, 14, 21, 24
Digital format, 28
Digital, 103-111
Director, 15
Disadvantages, 40
Directed generalization, 59
Disconnection, 72
Disengagement, 50
Distraction, 73

E
Element, 16
Email, 83-91
Electronic, 113-121
Ethical, 5
Explanation, 13

Experiment, 13, 27
Evaluation 18,

F
Facilitate, 15
Feedback, 13, 27
Focus, 27
Funding, 40

G
Gaps, 13
Global, 3
Glossary, 67
Goal, 17
Graph, 15
Grant, 16
Goal, 17
Guide, 3
Guidebook, 57

H
Historical internet, 4, 5, 34
Hypothesis, 4,5, 10, 20, 75

I
Illustrations, 42, 85
Information, 120

Inquiry, 5
Inservice, 9, 65
Instruction, 37
Internet, 3-11
Internet Problems, 4, 10
Investigation, 4, 11
Issues, 8, 23, 39, 48
Itinerary, 13

J
Journal, 56

L
Limitation, 21
Link (s), 36
Literacy, 20
Literature review, 3, 33

M
Mission, 3

N
Network, 81
Noted, 114
Noteworthy, 104

O

Objective(s), 16, 34, 44, 47

Observations, 13-17

Online, 53-61

P

Participants, 11, 19, 33, 47, 119

Periodicals, 5

Pilot, 33

Philosophy, 81

Portal, 17

Principles, 14

Problem Solving, 19

Procedures, 17

Professional development, 13

Prospectus, 44

Purpose, 5, 29, 37

Q

Queries, 23

Questions, 6, 23

Questionnaire, 23

R

Rationale, 20

Research design, 6

Research theories, 6

Research, 4, 21, 23-30, 33, 118

Resources, 13

Response (s), 7, 11, 13, 63

Revamping, 23

Review, 15

Rubrics, 4

S

Schedule, 17

Security, 30

Solution (s) ,11, 54

Sources, 15

Staff, 48

Strategies, 19

Status, 20

Subjects, 4

Strength, 26, 116

Summary, 16

Support, 79

Subjects, 3

Survey, 4, 27, 28

Syllabus, 24

T

Teams, 16

Technology, 13-21

Test Analysis, 29

Theme, 7
Thesis, 21
Timeline, 3
Tools, 61
Topics, 10

U
Utilized, 61
University, 27, 69, 71, 79

V
Virtual, 63-71
Vision, 13
Visual, 46

W
Weakness, 8, 59
Web, 23-31
Websites, 25, 26
Workable, 69

Y
Year, 91

AFTERWORD

Having been an educational writer for years I know the professional demands placed on my time to write. With the development of more technology and computer emphasis in most fields there is a need for a digital type of phrase book to help modernize some research thoughts and phrases. The **Digital Research Phrase Book** has focused on a variety of ideas that encompass online principles, internet, electronic digital, cyber, technology, data, web based, virtual, email and computer topics. By incorporating more digital phrases into research writing there can be more of a shift to connect to the world of technology.

www.ingramcontent.com/pod-product-compliance
Lightning Source LLC
Chambersburg PA
CBHW021832020426
42334CB00014B/587